# HOLIDAY WRAPPING PAPER

## Adult & Children's Coloring Book

## Series, Book 2

## America Selby

©Copyrighted Material
A Ladies Image Publishing
americaselby@outlook.com

Dear Coloring Enthusiast,

Thank you so much for choosing my book. I know you will completely enjoy coloring these beautiful pages.

When coloring, it is very helpful if you place thicker paper or card behind the page. This helps with bleed-through and also helps you stay focused on that page's art.

Whether you purchased this coloring book or were given the book as a gift you will find coloring very beneficial in many different ways. Regardless of the reasons for starting this fun and relaxing hobby you will soon see that you are reaping several mental health benefits.

These include experiencing a stronger sense of focus, and a more finely tuned sense of vision and motor skills. In the end, no matter why you choose to take up coloring as an adult, you will find yourself training your brain and fine tuning your mental clarity, while at the same time placing yourself in a wonderfully relaxed state.

Enjoy,

*America Selby*

Copyright © 2016 – Holiday Wrapping Paper Illustrations

All rights reserved. This book may not be reproduced in whole or part, without written permission from the publisher. The exception is by a reviewer who may color a few pages for a review. Not any part of the book can be reproduced, stored in a retrieval system, or transmitted in any form or by any means electronic, mechanical, photocopying, recording, or other, without written permission from the publisher.

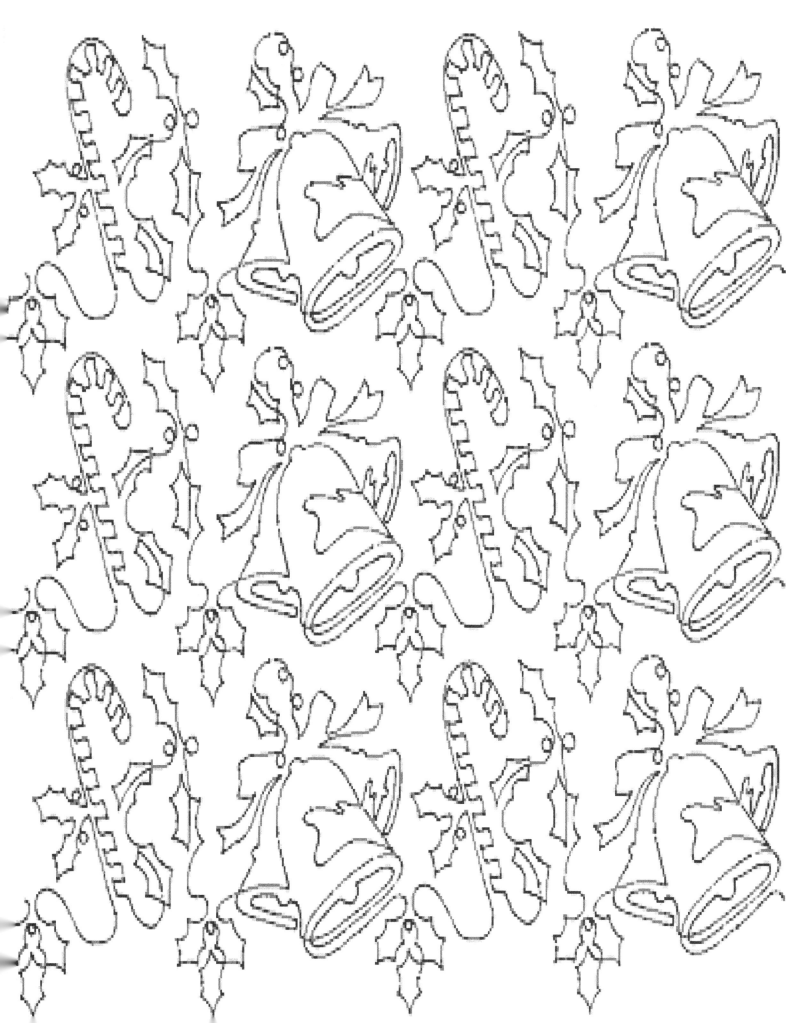

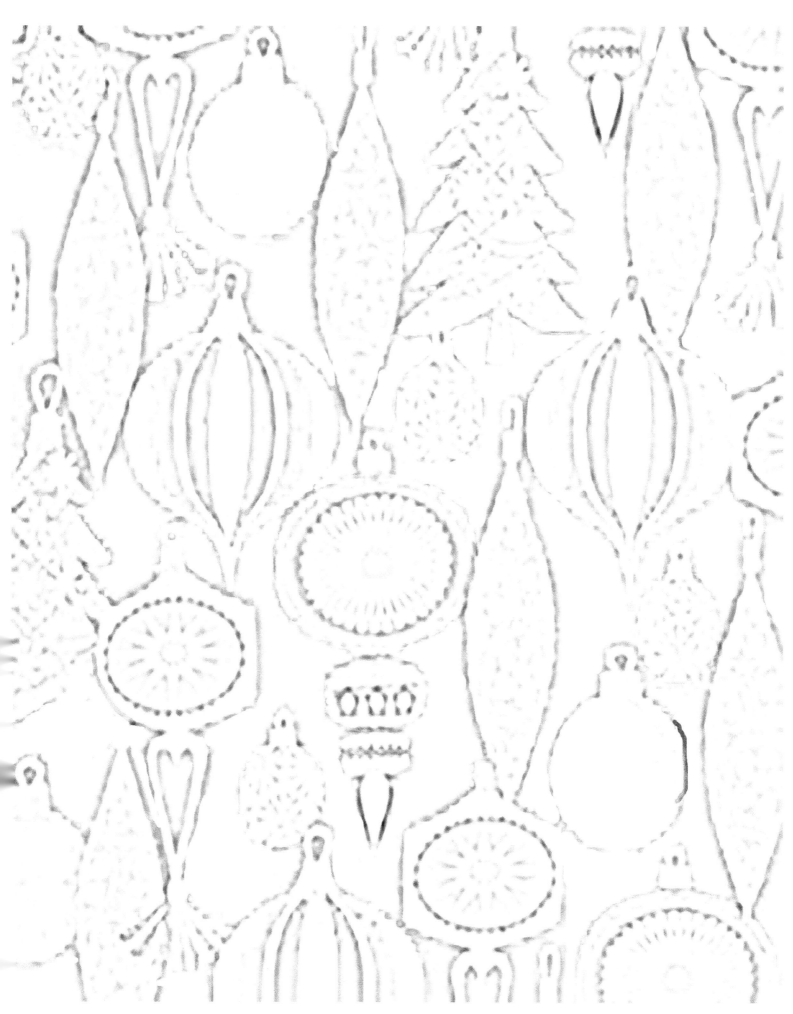

Please leave a review and copies of the pictures you have colored, I would love to see them. Go to amazon.com and type in America Selby to find my books.

# Enjoy some of my other books.

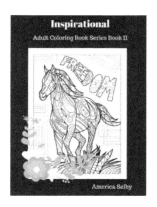

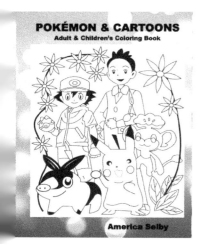

# Vintage Holiday
## Adult Coloring Book

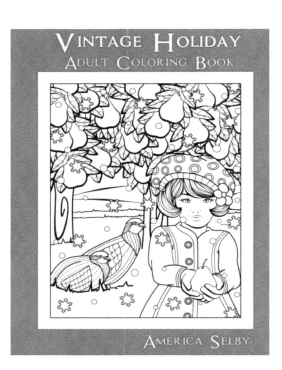

America Selby

Printed in the USA
CPSIA information can be obtained
at www.ICGtesting.com
LVHW080422110724
785188LV00005B/317